Contents

2 Introduction
4 Bursting with colour
6 Crumpled colours
8 The blushing bride
10 Zany zebra
12 Scissored snakes
14 Fringe benefits
16 Folding flakes
18 Pleated people
20 Threading puppets
22 Sew and stitch
24 Sticky farm
26 Model magic
28 Wonky walls
30 Making holes
32 Skills development chart

Introduction

Developing skills

When we think of the relevance of constructing and making to children in the Foundation Stage, we often see only a creative activity and fail to realize fully its importance in the teaching and introduction of fundamental manipulative skills. It is a common mistake to assume that children somehow acquire these important skills as they go along.

To construct something involves a process of many small steps. We need to break down these steps and introduce them individually to children so that they are able to master them properly and therefore produce finished products of quality. When we actively teach children how to cope with cutting, gluing, sticking, folding, tearing and crumpling, there is an immediate improvement in the standard of their work, and subsequently the children's confidence and self-esteem increase.

This book provides a series of activities which show the early years practitioner how to help young children to develop their constructing and making skills. The activities included provide a focus for particular skills such as tearing, crumpling, snipping and cutting, and at the same time providing ideas for enjoyable constructing and making tasks.

When young children are cutting, folding, sticking and gluing, they are developing many essential skills that they require for future life as well as practising hand–eye co-ordination and developing manual dexterity.

Early Learning Goals

Constructing and making provides a programme that helps children towards achieving the Early Learning Goals identified by the Qualifications and Curriculum Authority. The children are provided with opportunities to work together and support each other as a group, and through this, their personal, social and emotional development is advanced. They begin to share equipment, taking turns and becoming increasingly sensitive to the feelings of others.

The children's knowledge and understanding of the world develops as they are provided with opportunities to ask questions about why things happen and how things work. The activities also provide them with opportunities to build and construct with a wide range of familiar and new objects and resources.

Physical development is improved as the children develop the dexterity to handle tools such as scissors and construction toys appropriately and with increasing control. They are taught how to use tools and materials safely to prevent themselves or others from being hurt.

As the children progress through these adult-led activities, they are developing a skills-base which they can utilize in their own creative development and exploration of shape, form and space in two and three dimensions.

Baseline Assessment

The activities in this book are focused around developing skills in young children that will enable them to achieve aspects of the Early Learning Goals in the six areas of learning during the Foundation Stage. This will allow them to confidently tackle the Baseline Assessment tasks that they will be expected to complete as they enter Reception in mainstream school.

How to use this book

This book aims to demonstrate how you can introduce and develop constructing and making skills with young children through many fun activities. Each activity concentrates on a new skill or an advanced level of a skill previously introduced. The activities provided are stepping-stones that the children can develop further when incorporating them into their own creative ideas.

The activities are designed to be used according to the children's level of development. The photocopiable activity sheet that goes with each task aims to consolidate learning and also provides a record of each child's individual achievement.

All of the activities are adult-directed and require the presence and interaction of an adult. It is therefore important that the activities are incorporated into the planning procedures of individual settings and that the adult leading the activity is fully prepared and aware of the purpose and desired outcome of each activity.

Progression

The activities in the book have been devised to ensure a gradual progression and build-up of skills. Each activity has one main skill focus but may use a variety of previously encountered skills to enable the children to complete their practical task. For example, the first activity in the book requires the children to concentrate on the new skill of tearing, but a small amount of gluing is also required, although it is not the main focus of the activity.

Home links

Parents and carers are a valuable resource in any classroom and should be encouraged wherever possible to become involved in their children's learning. Invite them into your setting to work alongside you, regularly inform them of their children's progress and achievements, and encourage them to practise skills at home with their children by using the 'Home link' activity suggestions.

Bursting with colour

Learning objective
To develop co-ordination and control through tearing skills.

Group size
Five children.

What you need
A copy of the photocopiable sheet for each child and one for yourself; coloured tissue paper; glue; *The Hedgehog's Balloon* by Nick Butterworth (Collins Picture Lions) or a story about balloons.

Preparation
Cut the tissue paper into squares of approximately 20cm to make tearing more manageable for the children.

What to do
Read *The Hedgehog's Balloon* and talk about it with the children. Ask them if they like playing with balloons – what games do they play? Look at the balloon outlines on the photocopiable sheet. Ask the children what colour they think the balloons might be and encourage them to suggest ways to make them more colourful, such as colouring or painting. Praise their ideas and explain that you will show them how to make the picture more colourful by adding a collage of tissue paper.

Choose some colourful tissue and show the children how to make accurate tearing movements. Place the thumb and index finger of each hand on either side of the line that you wish to tear, then rip only the area between these fingers.

Tear small stamp-sized squares and demonstrate to the children how to glue these inside the balloon outlines on the photocopiable sheet, arranging them edge to edge so that no white paper is showing.

Individual recording
Give each child a copy of the photocopiable sheet and invite them to choose some coloured tissue to begin tearing into small squares. Encourage the children to glue the squares accurately onto one of their balloon outlines to give a slightly overlapping appearance while filling the balloon with colour. Use different-coloured tissue for each balloon.

Support
Enlarge the photocopiable sheet and provide larger pieces of torn paper for younger children. Cut their balloon pictures out for them.

Extension
When older children have completed their picture, allow them to cut around their balloon outlines and glue them onto blue sugar paper. Add thick wool or twine for the strings.

Assessment
Check for small regular-shaped pieces of torn paper, which show accuracy and consistency in tearing. As the children become more skilled, their torn shapes will become more uniform and regular in size and shape.

Home links
Ask parents and carers to help their children practise tearing skills by drawing an outline for their child to fill using torn pieces of magazines and newspapers.

Bursting with colour

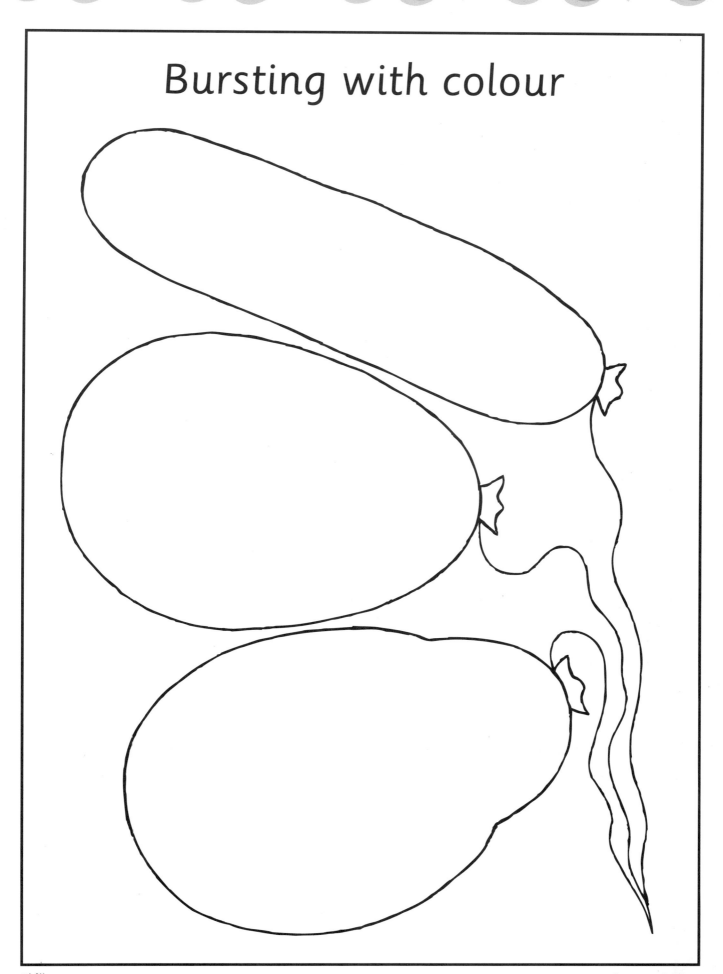

Crumpled colours

Learning objective
To explore how the texture, shape and form of paper can be changed to give an attractive decorative effect for craftwork.

Group size
Five children.

What you need
A copy of the photocopiable sheet for each child; newspaper; tissue paper; glue.

Preparation
Cut a selection of coloured tissue paper into small squares of approximately 5cm.

What to do
Tell the children that you are going to play a game to see who can throw balls of crumpled newspaper into a waste-paper basket. Encourage each child to make a large ball and a small ball. Talk about how we can make the balls smaller and larger by varying the force with which we squeeze the paper. Notice how the appearance of the paper has changed from being flat to three-dimensional. Tell the children that they have experienced crumpling, which is a craft technique that gives two-dimensional squares of paper an interesting three-dimensional textured appearance.

Show the children the pre-cut squares of paper and talk about their shape and texture. Ask the children to roll the paper into balls. Encourage them to use their fingers and thumbs to roll the paper, giving them greater manipulative skills than if they use the palms of their hands. Look at the balls of tissue that they have created and draw their attention to the texture of the paper and the way that it has taken on a three-dimensional appearance. Are the balls similar in size or do they vary?

Individual recording
Give each child a copy of the photocopiable sheet with the outline drawing of a flower and ask them to make it more colourful and three-dimensional by gluing crumpled coloured tissue paper onto it. Suggest trying to make small dense balls of tissue for the centre of the flower with larger looser balls for the petals and leaves.

Support
Let younger children use bigger squares of tissue paper which make larger crumpled balls to cover areas more quickly.

Extension
Encourage older children to reinforce their tearing skills (from the previous activity) by tearing and crumpling their own squares of tissue.

Assessment
Look at the finished picture and consider how densely the balls of tissue have been glued onto the outline. Look at the size of the tissue balls and check for accuracy in the force used to crumple tissue. As the children's skills improve, the size and shape of the crumpled balls should become more uniform, and as they get more proficient they will be able to make more tissue balls and apply them in greater quantity.

Home links
Ask parents and carers to demonstrate to their children how to use two drinking straws and crumpled paper balls to play a game of 'Blow football' at home.

Crumpled colours

The blushing bride

Learning objective
To develop cutting skills to make small snipping movements while holding scissors correctly and safely.

Group size
Five children.

What you need
A copy of the photocopiable sheet for each child and one for yourself; child-safe scissors; an assortment of different-coloured paper, tissue or card; a wedding invitation or a wedding photograph showing confetti; glue sticks; newspaper.

Preparation
Cut the paper or card that you will be using into strips of approximately 2cm by 10cm to make them more manageable for the children when cutting. This also prevents wasting large amounts of paper.

What to do
Show the children a wedding invitation or some photographs of a wedding. Encourage them to share any experiences that they have of weddings. Show them a photograph of a bride having confetti thrown over her and discuss what is happening in the picture and why.

Provide each child with a copy of the photocopiable sheet. Explain that you would like them to cut confetti for the bride in the picture. Demonstrate how to hold scissors correctly and safely when cutting paper and when holding or passing them to a friend. Show the children how to cut small irregular pieces of paper from the strips that you have made. Give each child a strip of paper and encourage them to snip paper into small sections. When children initially begin to use scissors, this is naturally the first thing that they do, snipping small pieces of paper into continually smaller pieces.

Individual recording
Provide glue sticks for the children to spread glue roughly in and around the bride outline. Invite them to snip different-coloured paper over the glued sheet. The coloured chips will stick randomly on the paper.

Support
Younger children can use stiff card, which is easier to manoeuvre and makes snipping easier.

Extension
Older children can practise snipping tissue paper, which requires more skill in holding and manoeuvring the paper and the scissors.

Assessment
Look at the snippets of paper stuck onto the bride outline. Have they been cleanly cut or do they show evidence of tearing and pulling? Consider also the size and regularity of the snipped pieces – small regular shapes indicate more control.

Home links
Ask parents and carers to help their children to make a collage picture by sticking pieces of wedding confetti onto a piece of paper.

The blushing bride

Skills for early years Constructing and making

Photocopiable **9**

Zany zebra

Learning objective
To use scissors safely and confidently while making continuous cutting movements.

Group size
Four children.

What you need
A copy of the photocopiable sheet for each child and one for yourself; books or posters showing photographs of zebras; stiff black paper or card; scissors; glue.

What to do
Look at pictures of zebras and talk with the children about their colours and pattern. Explain that the black and white stripes enables them to hide more effectively in the long grass where they live.

Show the children the photocopiable sheet of the zebra shape. Does this animal look like a zebra? Compare it with the zebra photographs and point out the features that are shared by both. Ask, 'What is one main difference between this zebra and the ones that you have looked at?'.

Explain that you are going to make stripes for your zebras by cutting long thin strips from black paper or card. Demonstrate to the children how to cut carefully, making sure to hold the paper or card firmly.

Individual recording
Give each child a copy of the photocopiable sheet and encourage them to cut some stiff black paper or card into thin strips. Help the children to measure the length of the individual stripes needed for each part of the zebra. If necessary, help them to cut them to an appropriate length before gluing them on.

Support
Draw white lines onto the black paper or card with chalk to act as a guide for younger children's cutting.

Extension
Provide older children with a ruler and coloured pencil so that they can practise their ruling skills by drawing the lines onto the card or paper themselves.

Assessment
Check how skilled the children have been with their cutting. Look at the width of each stripe and consider how smooth an edge it has. As the children become more skilled, their cutting edge will be smoother and the stripes will be thinner.

Home links
Ask parents and carers to encourage their children to practise cutting out pictures at home.

Scissored snakes

Learning objective
To use scissors skilfully and with control to cut around curved and irregular shapes.

Group size
Four children.

What you need
The photocopiable sheet copied onto thin card for each child; scissors; thick coloured marker; black thread; sticky tape.

What to do
Cutting around curves and rounded shapes can be difficult for children to master. Demonstrate and explain to the children how to cut around curved objects by continually turning the card or paper and readjusting their thumb and forefinger grip of the hand holding the paper. The hand cutting the paper must continue to make smooth cutting movements around the desired shape.

Individual recording
Provide each child with the photocopiable sheet copied onto thin card. Explain that you would like them to cut the snake from the photocopiable sheet, following the dark outline, so that they have the circular snake shape on its own. Using a coloured marker, draw over the black spiral line up to the point where it joins the snake's head. Ask the children to carefully cut around this coloured line using the cutting technique that you demonstrated earlier. Emphasize the importance of cutting carefully and accurately in order to produce a complete snake. When the snake is cut into one long spiral, attach some thin black thread to its head and hang it from the ceiling. Let the children enjoy the way that it spins around.

Support
Encourage younger children to cut around the outline of the snake themselves but if necessary, help them with the spiralling.

Extension
Let older children practise cutting snakes of different widths and lengths. To make a long thin snake, which requires considerably more cutting skills, draw a snake for the children that is a much tighter spiral.

Assessment
Consider how well the children have coped with the cutting task. Look at how closely they have been able to follow the cutting line around the spiral. Have the children managed to cut a complete snake or was it cut short?

Home links
Provide the following instructions so that parents and carers can make pom-poms with their children.

Cut two discs of stiff card of equal size. Cut a smaller disc in the middle of each disc. Place the two main discs together and start to wind wool around them to make pom-poms. When it becomes difficult to wind wool through the middle, slip in scissors between the discs and cut the wool. Insert a piece of wool between the discs and tie tightly. Cut away the cardboard discs and fluff out the woollen pom-pom. Glue paper eyes and features to make a comical character.

Scissored snakes

Fringe benefits

Learning objective
To use complex folding and cutting skills to produce a decorative fringing effect.

Group size
Four children.

What you need
A copy of the photocopiable sheet for each child and one for yourself; brightly-coloured crêpe paper; scissors; coloured pens; glue.

Preparation
Cut the top edge from a roll of coloured crêpe paper to make a long strip approximately 10cm wide. Unroll the crêpe paper that you have cut and refold it over onto itself in lengths of approximately 15cm, so that the strip is several layers of paper thick. Pepare another three strips.

What to do
Give each child a copy of the photocopiable sheet and talk about the head outline on the paper. Ask the children to identify what features are missing from the face. Invite them to draw on the missing features – eyes, nose, mouth, eyebrows and eyelashes. When the children have finished drawing the features, discuss what else is missing. Talk about different hair-styles and how they could create an effective hair-style on their picture.

Individual recording
Explain to the children that they are going to give their characters hair by cutting paper using a technique that is called fringing. Allow each child to choose a folded strip of paper from the selection that you have prepared. Demonstrate how to create fringing by making controlled cuts up the folded paper, stopping short of cutting through it completely. When cutting is complete, carefully unwind the fringing. Show the children how to arrange the fringing to make different hair-styles and how to cut some of the length of the fringe if they want to make shorter styles. Help them to glue the fringing onto the photocopiable sheet.

Support
Using a thick marker pen, draw guidelines onto younger children's strips of paper.

Extension
Encourage older children to try to make double-edged fringing or fringing with a patterned or scalloped edge.

Assessment
Encourage the children to repeat the fringing activity without any adult guidance to produce a large class face with many strands of fringed hair. Check if the children are cutting in straight lines and that they remember to stop short of cutting all the way through the paper.

Home links
Ask parents and carers to practise fringing techniques at home, helping their children to make fringes that can be glued to an empty baby milk tin or similar, to make an attractive pencil holder.

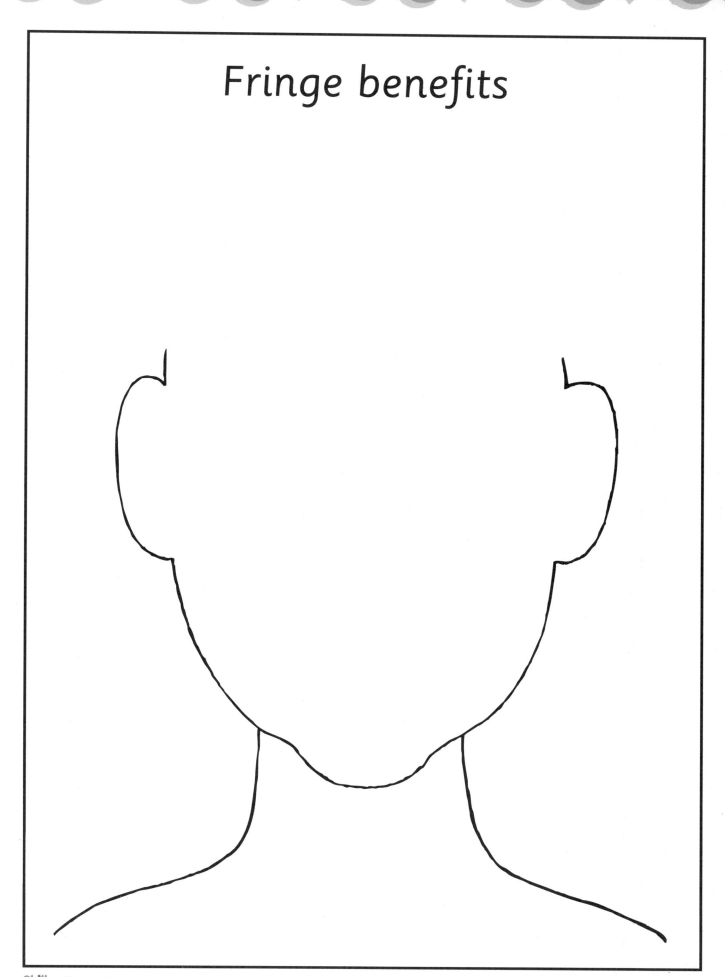

Folding flakes

Learning objective
To make accurate folds and use cutting skills to good decorative effect.

Group size
Four children.

What you need
A copy of the photocopiable sheet for each child; discs of paper; scissors; glue sticks; glitter; pictures of snow scenes and landscapes; picture of a magnified snowflake.

Preparation
Cut discs approximately 15cm in diameter from good quality paper – thin newsprint-type paper is not suitable as it is too difficult for the children to handle.

What to do
Many young children find it very difficult to make accurate folds. This activity provides an opportunity for them to practise folding and snipping to make an attractive snowflake. Show the children pictures or photographs of snow scenes and landscapes. Discuss times that they may have seen snow. Have any of them ever seen a lot of snow like in the pictures? Show the children a photograph of a single snowflake that has been magnified to show its shape and form.

Individual recording
Give each child a paper disc. Show them how to fold it exactly in half. Emphasize that it is important that the edges of the circle meet and do not overlap. Demonstrate how to run your fingers along the fold to make it sharp. Ask the children to copy what you have done to make their own 'rocker' shape. Now demonstrate how to fold the paper over on itself again to form a triangle with one curved edge, resembling a piece of pie. Finally, fold the quartered circle over on itself once more. Each time emphasize the importance of making the edges meet and the fold sharp.

When the folding is complete, show the children how to snip off the point of the folded paper. Now snip some shapes into each edge of the folded paper. Explain that you must not over-cut or the paper will fall to pieces! When cutting is complete, carefully open out the circle and watch the snowflake appear.

Let the children decorate the snowflakes with glue and glitter. Give each child a copy of the photocopiable sheet and invite them to stick their snowflake onto the snow scene.

Support
Let younger children make less intricate snowflakes with only two folds to quarter the circle.

Extension
Invite older children to try to experiment with different types of paper, such as tissue to make translucent snowflakes for the window, or foil and coloured Cellophane.

Assessment
Look at how accurately the children fold and crease their paper. Check if they work independently after the initial instructions.

Home links
Ask parents and carers to repeat the snowflake activity at home with their children using a larger circle of paper to make an attractive doily or place mat for a party tea.

Folding flakes

Skills for early years Constructing and making

Pleated people

Learning objective
To show increasing control and accuracy in making paper folds.

Group size
Four children.

What do you need
A copy of the photocopiable sheet for each child; a collection of objects with pleats such as a pleated skirt, lampshade and paper fan; coloured paper; glue; newspaper.

Preparation
Cut the coloured paper into strips of approximately 30cm by 12cm and 30cm by 2cm.

What to do
Gather the children together and ask them to look at the displayed collection of objects. Talk about each one and discuss whether there are any features that the objects have in common. Draw the children's attention towards the fact that all of these things have been pleated. Explain that pleating is a special way of folding. To pleat paper or material of any sort, we must make folds which go in one direction and then the other.

Demonstrate to the children how to pleat a strip of paper to make a concertina shape with approximately 2cm between each fold. Use the method of turning the paper over between each fold and ensure you verbalize the movements to help the children to remember the technique – for instance, 'fold and turn, fold and turn…' and so on.

Give the children a piece of newspaper and help them to fold it into pleats. It may help to work together as a group with everyone making the fold and turn at the same time while an adult supervises very closely.

Individual recording
When the children have finished their pleating, give each child a copy of the photocopiable sheet and ask them to pleat a body to stick onto the person. Let the children select colours of their choice from paper that has been pre-cut into thin strips for the arms and wide strips for the body. Stick the pleated strips onto the sheet.

Support
Let younger children make wider pleats with three to four centimetres between each fold.

Extension
Encourage older children to add cut-out or drawn hand shapes to the end of their person's concertina'd arms.

Assessment
Look at how carefully the children have folded the paper. Look for a smaller width of pleats and folding which is straight and well pronounced.

Home links
Ask parents and carers to make paper fans with their children from coloured wrapping paper.

Pleated people

Threading puppets

Learning objective
To use hand–eye co-ordination in threading activities.

Group size
Four children.

What you need
Several copies of the photocopiable sheet; variety of pasta; beads; cotton reels; thread or laces; sticky tape; cardboard tubes; string.

Preparation
Provide enough copies of the photocopiable sheet to give a reasonable choice of heads for each child's puppet. Stiffen the ends of all the laces and threads, either by dipping them in glue and leaving to dry or by winding sticky tape tightly round the end of the thread.

What to do
Give the children a variety of cotton reels, beads, macaroni and other pasta shapes and allow them to play with these shapes threading them onto string or laces. Demonstrate how to hold the thread or lace near the end, between the thumb and forefinger, and how to line up the end of the thread with the hole in the bead or pasta and push it gently through.

Individual recording
Give each child a cardboard tube and explain that they are going to make a puppet. Encourage the children to choose a head and a tail from their photocopiable sheets and cut them out. Help them to attach these to each end of their tube.

Make strings of beads or pasta to attach to the puppets as legs. Assist the children in draping one finished and tied string of beads in half over the back end of their cardboard tubes and securing this with sticky tape. Secure a second string onto the front end of each tube to give the puppets four dangling legs. Attach a piece of string to the centre of the tube with sticky tape and make the puppets dance.

Support
Provide larger-holed beads and pasta for younger children, as well as thicker laces with a well-stiffened end.

Extension
Older children can use a plastic needle and finer thread with small glass or plastic beads.

Assessment
Can the children confidently thread beads or macaroni onto a lace without any adult help? Consider the amount of threading that has been done in the time available. Also consider how intricately the skill has been applied and account for the levels of difficulty between large pasta tubes and fine glass beads.

Home links
Explain to parents and carers how to dye pasta with food colouring and let it dry before threading it with their children to make colourful pieces of jewellery.

Design Template

IMPORTANT - Ensure drawings are in **PORTRAIT FORMAT** and are **WITHIN THE LINES**. Make sure any text on the design is within the arrows. Only use felt tip pens or coloured pencils. We recommend teachers fill in the details to ensure correct names are printed on the final card.

www.myschoolprinting.co.uk

CHILD NAME

CLASS NAME

← Any text should be **ABOVE** this arrow

Any text should be **ABOVE** this arrow →

← Any text should be **BELOW** this arrow

Any text should be **BELOW** this arrow →

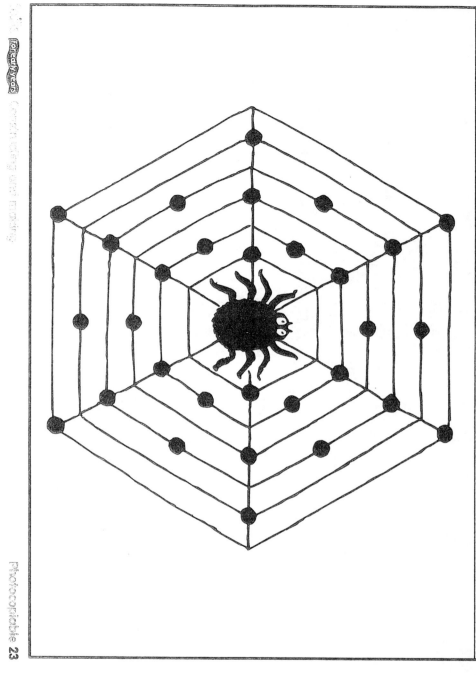

Threading puppets

Skills for early years Constructing and making

Threading puppets

Skills for early years Constructing and making

Photocopiable 21

Threading puppets

Sew and stitch

Learning objective
To become familiar with and carry out basic sewing techniques.

Group size
Four children.

What you need
The photocopiable sheet for each child copied onto thick card (laminated if possible); coloured wool; single hole-punch; glue or sticky tape; needles; thread; fabric.

Preparation
Using a single hole-punch, make holes on the copies of the photocopiable sheets as indicated to create a sewing card. Ensure that the ends of all laces and threads have been stiffened, either by dipping them in glue and letting them dry or by winding sticky tape tightly around the end of the thread.

What to do
Introduce the children to basic sewing. Discuss with them how sewing can be used to join two pieces of material together and also how it has a decorative use in embroidery. Help them to look for examples of stitching on their own clothing.

Show the children how to make the basic sewing movement of a running stitch. Demonstrate this on a large piece of material contrasting with the colour of the thread to make a large running stitch. Emphasize the repetition of your movements and encourage the children to chant in their heads 'up and down' or 'in and out'.

Individual recording
Give each child a sewing card and encourage them to sew coloured wool through the holes to make an attractive pattern.

Support
Punch fewer holes in the sewing cards and make them in a linear pattern so that younger children can easily follow along the holes using their running stitch without getting tangled.

Extension
Increase the number of holes all over the card and encourage older children to try to sew attractive patterns of crossing stitches. Alternatively, number the holes on the sewing card and ask the children to sew through the holes in the correct order.

Assessment
Follow the run of the stitches on the cards to check whether the children have grasped the in and out of the sewing stitch. Some children will have become confused and started making looping stitches and tangles around the card. If you have numbered the holes on the card, you will be able to check at a glance whether a child has followed the sequence correctly.

Home links
Encourage parents and carers to try sewing with their children at home.

Sew and stitch

Sticky farm

Learning objective
To select gluing materials and use them appropriately to complete a variety of tasks.

Group size
Four children.

What you need
A copy of the photocopiable sheet for each child and one for yourself; small-world farm; glue sticks; pot of PVA glue and spreaders; sticky tape and scissors; straw; seeds.

What to do
Use your small-world farm to introduce animals, buildings and machinery associated with farms. Allow the children ten minutes to play with the equipment and as they do, discuss where the animals live and what they like to eat.

Share the farm picture on the photocopiable sheet with the children. Use your own copy of the sheet to cut out the animals from the strip on the side. Talk with the children about where to place these animals on the photocopiable sheet.

Show the children three common types of sticking materials – a push-up glue stick, a pot of PVA glue and a roll of sticky tape. Talk with the children about the appropriateness of each of these to the task of sticking. Demonstrate how to use the glue stick by dabbing it sparingly onto the back of one of the pictures. Next, cut a small square of sticky tape to join another picture to the farm scene, and finally explain that the PVA glue is most effective for sticking large areas of straw or seeds onto the picture. Show the children how to use the spreader to place the glue on the correct areas of the picture.

Individual recording
Give each child a copy of the photocopiable sheet and ask them to cut the strip of animals from the side of the sheet and then cut neatly around them, as close to the outline as they can. Encourage them to glue loose materials such as seeds and short strands of straw onto large ground areas of the picture using the PVA glue. Let them stick two of their animals onto the picture using the glue stick and two of them using the sticky tape.

Support
Cut the animals out for younger children so that they can concentrate on their sticking.

Extension
Older children can practise their cutting skills before gluing the animals to the page.

Assessment
Check if the picture has been securely stuck, but without excess glue or tape. How neat is the overall appearance of the picture?

Home links
Ask parents and carers to try using household ingredients such as rice, pasta, lentils and so on to make an attractive glued collage at home with their children.

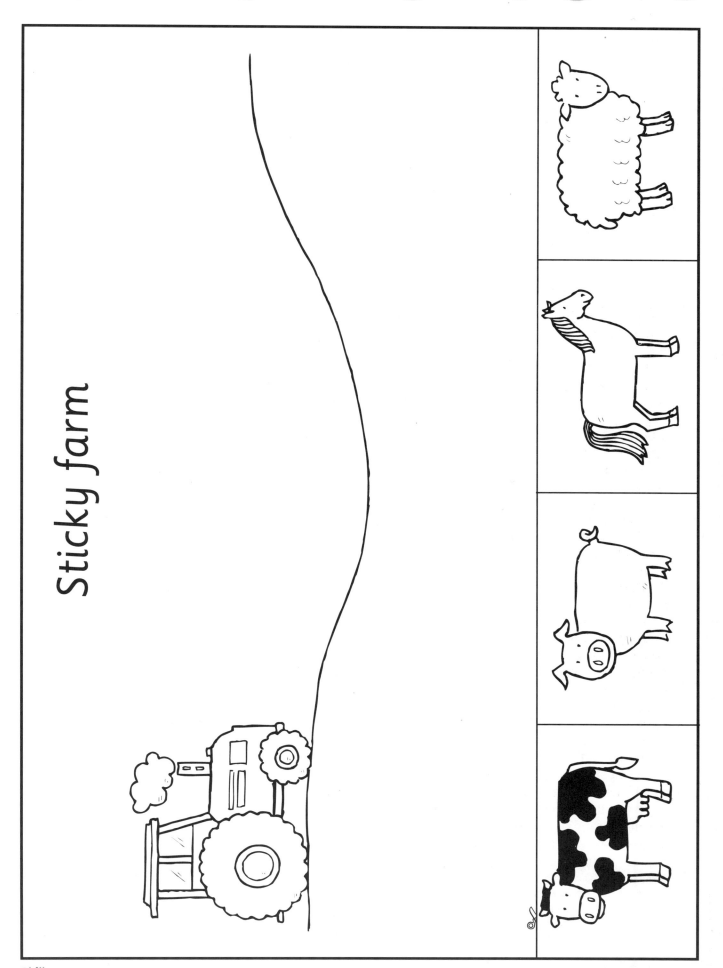

Model magic

Learning objective
To select the equipment needed to assemble and join together a variety of materials.

Group size
Four children.

What you need
A copy of the photocopiable sheet for each child; junk materials; glue; sticky tape.

Preparation
Ensure that you have enough boxes of various shapes and sizes in order to build the model illustrated on the photocopiable sheet. If you have time, turn your boxes inside out and glue them back together with a hot-glue gun. This will make them easier to paint and more absorbent for the glue and will also provide a plain surface to decorate.

What to do
Children who have used glue to make two-dimensional sticking pictures will often be of the opinion that glue will stick everything together. But when faced with making three-dimensional models, the children can become frustrated with the realization that this is not necessarily the case. Give the group lots of junk modelling materials and allow ten minutes to play freely with them. Discuss the models that they have made. If they have not used any of the materials, ask them why they chose not to. Talk about problems that have been encountered, asking questions such as 'Why do the cardboard tubes on the models keep falling over?' and 'Why will the glue not work on plastic containers?'.

Demonstrate how to fringe the edge of a cardboard tube and fold it out to make a flat surface for gluing. Show how to stick plastic cartons onto cardboard boxes with sticky tape.

Individual recording
Give each child a copy of the photocopiable sheet and provide a selection of the materials, sticky tape and glue needed to build the model illustrated on the photocopiable sheet. Ask the children to make the model, taking into consideration the sticking techniques that you have just demonstrated.

Support
Provide adult help for younger children with the fringing and taping process.

Extension
Give older children a selection of boxes and ask them to use all of them in their own design.

Assessment
Consider how appropriately the children have chosen the particular method of sticking and how well they have applied the techniques shown. How closely does the model represent the one illustrated on the photocopiable sheet?

Home links
Ask parents and carers to make a collection of household junk and to encourage their children to make a model house or car using as many boxes as possible.

Model magic

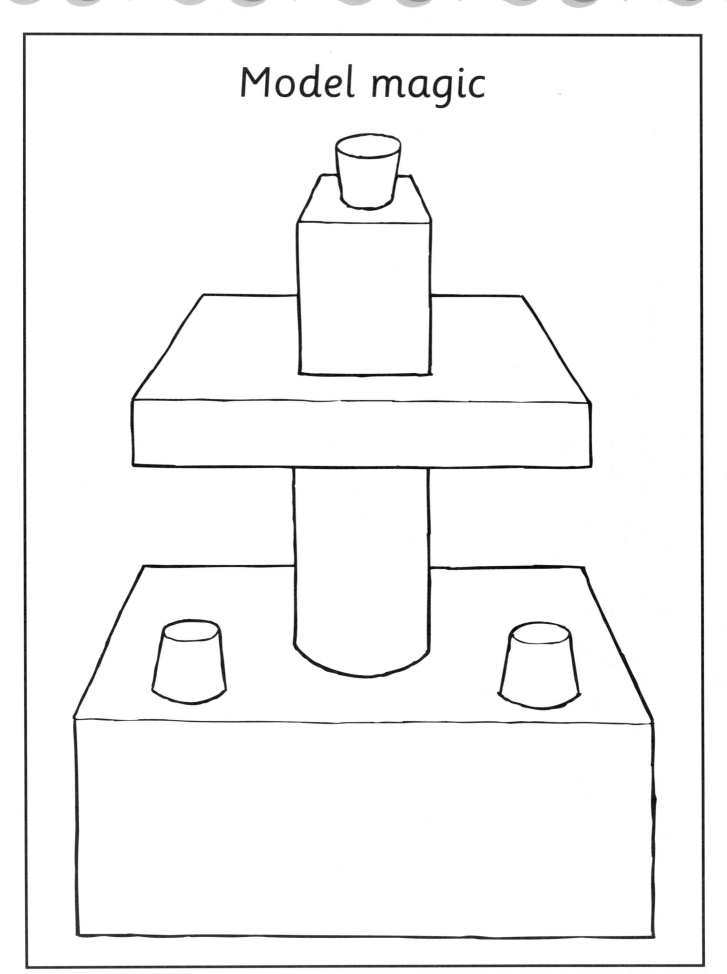

Wonky walls

Learning objective
To use building bricks to form a safe and strong construction.

Group size
Four children.

What you need
A copy of the photocopiable sheet for each child and one for yourself; Duplo bricks (or similar); sugar paper; scissors; glue.

Preparation
Cut out and colour the finger puppet from your copy of the photocopiable sheet. Cut out the two finger holes to make it into a puppet.

What to do
Show the children the Humpty Dumpty finger puppet that you have made. Give them a selection of Duplo bricks and ask them to work together to build a wall for Humpty to sit on. Children will generally stack bricks one on top of another; let them continue in this manner for a few minutes to allow them to practise placing the bricks carefully. Afterwards, show them how to build using a traditional brickwork pattern. Encourage them to work together again to build a second wall in this manner. Let them continue building like this until they are satisfied with their wall.

Look at the two walls which have been built and discuss which is the best and safest. Dismantle the unsafe wall and use the bricks to make the strong wall higher.

Individual recording
Give each child a copy of the photocopiable sheet and ask them to colour in the sheets and cut out the brick shapes. Encourage them to use these shapes to copy and record the pattern of the wall that you have just made. Each child can stick their brick shapes onto sugar paper with their Humpty Dumpty on the top of the wall.

Support
Cut out the bricks from the photocopiable sheet or use pre-cut sticky-paper shapes for younger children.

Extension
Ask older children to record their brick-building pattern by drawing around the bricks that they have used onto large sheets of sugar paper.

Assessment
Check whether the children are consistent in their building pattern and if they manage to consistently place the bricks evenly. Look carefully at whether they have managed to record the pattern correctly and neatly.

Home links
Ask parents and carers to remind their children to save the eggshell the next time that they have a boiled egg, and to help them carefully draw a face on it. They can fill the empty eggshell with damp cotton wool and cress seeds and watch their egghead as it grows green hair.

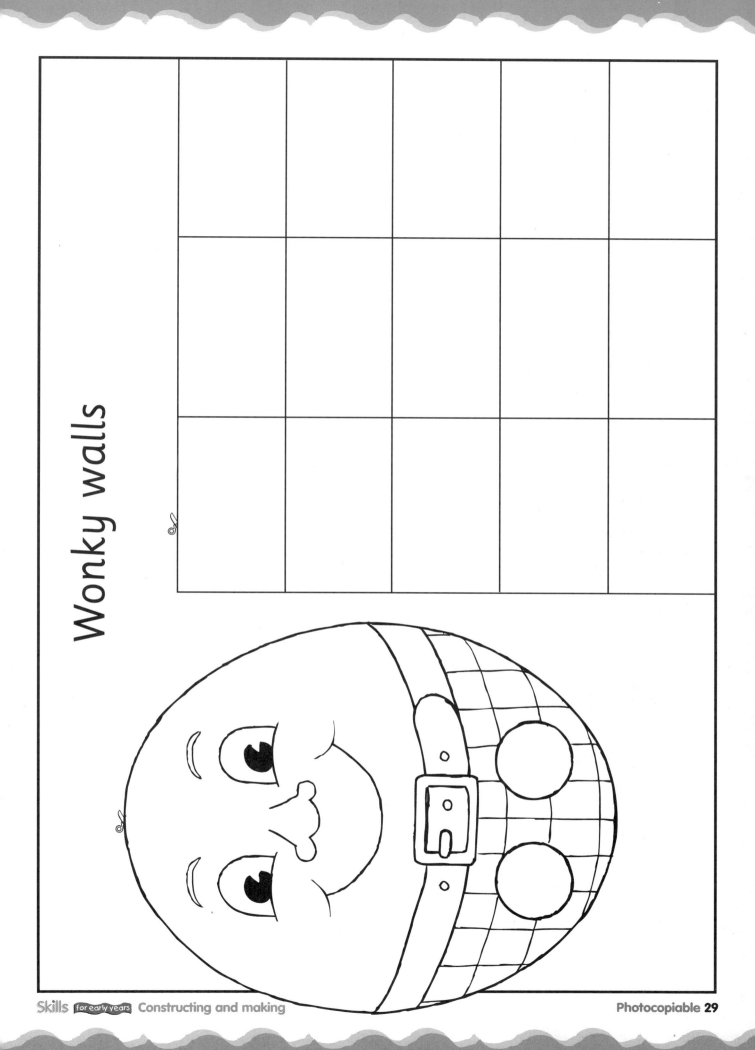

Making holes

Learning objective
To become familiar with new tools and use them appropriately and safely.

Group size
Four children.

What you need
A copy of the photocopiable sheet on thin card for each child; hole-punch; pencil sharpener; dowelling; pencil; coloured pencils; Plasticine; coloured wool; glue; scissors.

Preparation
Ensure that the Plasticine is soft and in a large malleable lump.

What to do
When constructing and making, it is essential that the children pierce holes in paper or card safely. There are two different ways of making holes, each way being appropriate for different types of task.

Firstly, demonstrate how to pierce a hole in paper or card by placing it firmly on top of a large lump of soft Plasticine. Hold the point of a pencil or dowelling on top of the object and carefully but firmly press down. The point should safely embed itself in the Plasticine and if the Plasticine is soft there is no danger of the object skidding on the hard surface underneath. The second way is to use a hole-punch. Demonstrate to the children how to use this and guide them in trying it themselves. Explain that this kind of machine makes larger holes that are better if you need to thread things through them.

Individual recording
Give each child a copy of the photocopiable sheet and ask them to colour the sections of the spinner shape differently and cut it out. Encourage them to use a sharpened piece of dowelling or a sharp pencil to make a small hole in the centre of the spinner onto Plasticine, pushing the dowelling half-way through the card to make a spinning top.

To practise using the hole-punch, give each child a paper plate and ask them to make holes along the top edge of the plate using the punch. Ask them to thread and tie pieces of coloured wool through the holes to make hair, then to cut out and colour the facial features of their choice from their photocopiable sheet and glue them onto the plate to make a face.

Support
Younger children will need help and close supervision when piercing holes with dowelling and when using a hole-punch.

Extension
Encourage older children to create a larger number of holes on the paper plate with the hole-punch. Emphasize the need to position the hole-punch carefully as the number of holes increases.

Assessment
Check whether the children can confidently and safely punch holes by following the instructions outlined above.

Home links
Ask parents and carers to help their children to make patterns with a small hole-punch. They could make hole patterns on sheets of paper and experiment with what happens if you fold paper and then punch holes in it.

Making holes

Name _____

Skills development chart

- I can make controlled tears using my thumbs and forefingers.
- I can apply crumpled paper to make a 3D effect.
- I can accurately thread objects onto laces.
- I can sew in a running stitch motion.
- I can make accurate folds to create pleated effects in paper.
- I can use glue accurately and effectively.
- I can hold scissors correctly and make snipping movements.
- I can make accurate folds in paper.
- I can choose an appropriate sticking medium for a task.
- I can use scissors to cut in a straight line.
- I can punch holes using a hole-punch or piercing method.
- I can use building bricks to make a bonded construction.
- I can use scissors accurately to make decorative fringing.
- I can use scissors to cut around corners and curves.